Word Art
Of the Garifuna Spirit

A collection of spirit-filled poems and illustrations

Janet Guity-Sabio

Illustrations by: Victor Garcia

GARIPULSE
ENTERTAINMENT, LLC

Word Art of the Garifuna Spirit

By: Janet Guity-Sabio

ISBN-10: 0988522004

ISBN-13: 978-0-9885220-0-8

Printed in the United States of America

Table of Contents

Preface

Word Art of the Garifuna Spirit is a collection of writings inspired by the circumstances of my life of love, sadness, sacrifice, betrayal, discouragement, and ultimately triumph over adversity by responding with compassion and faith with the help of the Holy Spirit and the spirit of my Garifuna ancestors inspiring me to open my heart and soul from where these words of hope and encouragement emanate.

The strong spirit of my Garifuna ancestors is very much alive. It transcends time and space and it is with honor that I share with my readers my spirit-filled poetry.

About Me

I am the eighth of ten children raised by a Honduran mother who was widowed at a relatively young age. Eventually one by one and two by two, we all immigrated to the United States by the late 1960's. This was a time of turmoil and tremendous changes in America, but I did not understand the meaning of the civil rights events that I was living. Survival in this "new world" was my number one priority; enduring loneliness and rejection by not being able to speak English, not being "black enough" for some, or being "too black" for others. Sitting in a classroom in a totally unfamiliar setting resulted in a feeling of isolation, and at times despair.

I was fortunate to have a teacher, Mr. Donald Raynor, who cared and encouraged me during my very difficult first year of school in the USA. I also relied on the kindness of a few of the Spanish-speaking students to help me navigate the classroom instruction.

I learned from my mother the importance of having a strong work ethic. She showed me courage, how to embrace sacrifice, and that I should be my brother's and sister's keeper; but most of all, I learned about hope, and that no matter how tough things were, there will be a better tomorrow. Through perseverance and dreaming of living like "the Americans" I watched on television, I completed a university education and subsequently obtained the licensure in Certified Public Accountancy and achieved a diverse and successful career.

I experienced being loved and cherished by my husband Amilcar, followed by the joy of motherhood with the birth of our three magnificent sons Jeremy, Joshua and Joseph. The lessons learned from struggle and sacrifice prepared me to more effectively manage the pain and sadness of my husband's battle with a degenerative disease, to be compounded in subsequent years with my own battle with breast cancer, which I am happy to report I am winning.

Janet Guity- Sabio

Foreword

It is an extreme honor to have been asked to write the foreword to **Word Art of the Garifuna Spirit**. The name itself provoked in me many thoughts regarding what the book would be about. **Word Art of the Garifuna Spirit** is a very picturesque depiction of the author's journey into self-discovery and self-expression. The Words in the book come out of the experience of personal challenges that ultimately led to triumph over despair and sadness. The author is also inspired by the spirit of her Garifuna Ancestors; she is motivated by the desire to seek life's answers through a "Garicentric" perspective and the need to preserve the culture of the only Black Indigenous people in the Americas.

I have known Janet for many years and had not seen this unique, eclectic, and artistic side of her until she paid me the complement of asking me what I thought about a poem she was working on and read it to me. I was so touched by the way her poetry spoke to me. At the same time I realized that it would speak to others based on the similarity of life and human experiences, regardless of culture, ethnicity or race.

Word Art of the Garifuna Spirit is a lesson for us all in spiritually healthy living. Each poem in one way or another helps us to realize that we don't know what is inside of us until we are tested. Throughout Janet's experience with personal travails as well as illness in both her and her husband's family, she has allowed the Holy Spirit and the history of the ancestors to guide her in the creation of a beautiful collage of heart-wrenching poems of her experiences dealt to her in this life.

In "Should Have, Could Have Path", anyone who has suffered from the universal ailment of procrastination, and later regrets taking that path could certainly intimately relate. "Letting Go" paints and weaves the emotional roller coaster involved in losing someone you love and coming to terms with that loss. When I read "Garifuna Music" I could visualize the Garifuna villages and hear the drums beating rhythmically, I could also feel the warm ocean breeze and smell its warm sweet, alluring scent.

I thoroughly enjoyed reading these poems, the artwork was equally compelling and is in concert with each other; I think you will enjoy it too. I found myself feeling cleansed and rejuvenated through this emotional expression. Sit back, dear reader and relax, you are in for a treat!

Edna Marina Sabio, M.E.D

Acknowledgment

This book of poetry is dedicated to the memory of Salomon Guity, my father, one of the most successful Garifuna businessmen of his time. He was the General Manager of the largest department store in La Ceiba, the grateful grandson of Sabina Martinez, the loving son of Luciana Martinez, the love of his wife Esther Núñez de Guity, the doting and loving father of Vilma, Yolanda, Salomon, Noemi (R.I.P.), Roy, Freddy (R.I.P.), Maritza, Janet, Miguel Angel, Eduardo, Raul (R.I.P.), and Gloria.

This book also honors those courageous ancestors exiled to Roatan, off of the coast of modern day Honduras in 1797, they prospered and became founders of major Cities such as La Ceiba and the community of Santa Rosa de Aguan. My great grandparents Francisco Núñez and his life partner Matilde Gotay were the original Garifuna founders of the city La Ceiba, Honduras. My other great grandparents Policarpo Cacho and his wife Nazaria Ramos Cacho were the leading business family of the major Garifuna founded Settlement of Santa Rosa de Aguan.

This book additionally intends to honor the heroic Garifuna ancestors that were involved in the signing of the Peace Treaty of 1773 in Yurumein (St. Vincent) between the British and the Garifuna in their efforts to preserve our ancestral territory. The twenty Garifuna patriots who signed the treaty and merit historical recognition are Jean Baptiste, Dufonte Begot, Boyordell, Dirang, Joseph Chatoyer, Doucre Baramont, Lalime, Junior, Broca, Saioe, Francois Laron, Saint Laron, Anisette, Clement, Bigott, Simon, Lalime, Senior, Justin Baüamont, Matthieu, Jean Louis Pacquin, and Gadel Goibau.

Silence the mind, open the heart
and connect to the Higher Power

Prayer

Be still and elevate your mind and spirit to a state of being. Silence the mind, open the heart and connect to the Higher Power, to be comforted, and to be guided.

Surrendering to the most High, developing intimacy with self and the universe, not anxious, not worried, not doubting, not requesting, not expecting, just open to the unveiling of God's awesome plan.

Sitting, waiting and listening for the internal voice that will fill the self-worth tank and connect to the spirit of God.

...as an act of love,
it is now time to just let it go...

Letting Go

Most worthy of your absolute best, however, not willing or maybe unable to give me your unreserved best, has altered the love into an isolated recollection. Like warm winter clothing no longer needed at the dawn of spring, your alleged love, like the layering of clothing in the winter is not essential, like a mirage in the desert, it was simply a figment of the imagination, and it is time to just let it go.

The bittersweet memory of what could have been; a sacred love unappreciated and destroyed by the indifference of an arid soul burned to the core, unable to see, unable to feel, and unable to sense the dazzlingly light illuminating the corridor of life.

A soul in ruins, a spirit governed by ego, is now in a position for redemptive rebirth, and to honor the One who is his divine purpose has been fulfilled, as an act of love, it is now time to just let it go.

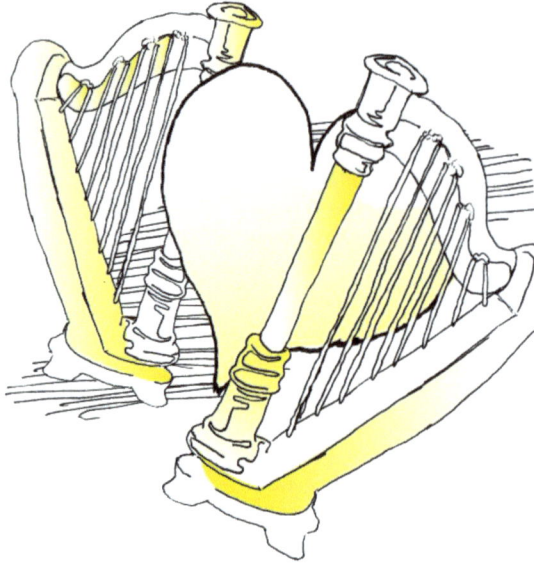

Looking for the pure and clear waters
from the fountain of inspiration

Essence of Inspiration

Looking for the pure and clear waters from the fountain of inspiration, the water that flows freely, quenching the thirst of the soul, searching for the right words to soothe the spirit of even just one person in the universe.

I do not ask for millions, thousands, or hundreds, just for the one, someone that would experience my message and make their heart sing!

The joy, peace, and love divinely inspired by the Most High would be transferred to that one being, the good vibrations of that one person would be transferred to another individual, and on and on until many would delight.

Touching millions of souls is up to the Most High, whom I trust, and has inspired me and has made my heart sing.

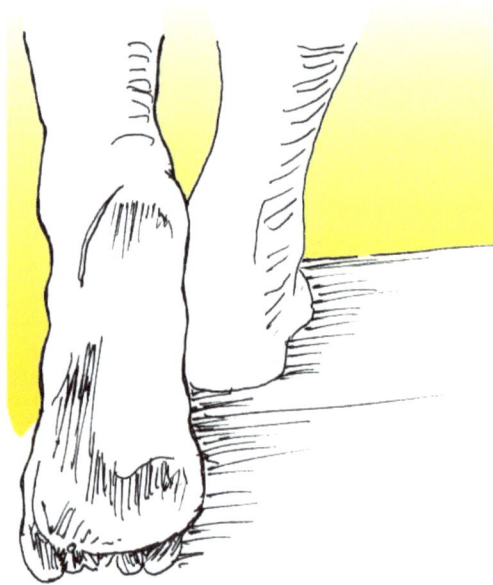

Granted the gift of discernment to
follow the path of Your divine plan

Offerings of the Creator

Granted the gift of discernment to follow the path of Your divine plan, turning into a fork in the road, used Your gift so mercifully granted to follow Your appointed path.

Granted the gift of patience to develop serenity and peace; embraced the spiritual fire that molds the character that evolved from charcoal into a brilliant diamond that illuminated the absence of light.

Granted a clear consciousness with eyes wide open, to see Your spirit in other people, ears in tune to the cry of those suffering in silence, a heart unhardened able to trust, open to love, and compassion.

Granted the gift of wisdom to evolve into the spiritual beings that You intended us to become; one with the universe, a devoted disciple, a fisher of people, a tool for the purpose of Your divine plan.

Technology has allowed us to be in touch with people
and visit distant places in a matter of seconds

Essence of Giving

Technology has allowed us to be in touch with people and visit distant places in a matter of seconds. We could pretend to be anyone we want, create fantasies that others see as real, as well as create an oasis in the perceived desert of our lives. But only by divine intervention through the power of love for another could it truly touch our hearts, and help us discover the God-given gifts that could be felt across time and distance.

Unable to see those gifts, unable to feel them, unable to give them out as intended, we implore God to help us discover the gifts granted.

Touch us with Your spirit to discover the purpose of what was so generously given us to confer away, so others could see You in us.

Touch us so we may have generosity of the spirit to give from the heart without expecting anything in return; but most importantly make us anonymous givers so as not to create any obligation.

That way we truly become what we were created to be, by the Indescribable, the Uncreated, the Self Existent, the Eternal, the All-Knowing source of all reality and being, God.

Pay attention to the inner voice, trust it

Should Have, Could Have Path

Living life unable to be taught, unable to take note, unable to create a vision due to the fear of being wrong, the fear of failure, the thought of one more letdown creates paralysis of action, remaining in the unending circle of "If I could have" syndrome, lost in the deceptive blueprint of the mind.

Embracing the spirit of God and the spirits of our ancestors, allows to move forward with the confidence of walking the right path, even when we come to a forked road and are unsure which way to go, choose a path, be it right or wrong. If guided by the spirit of the Most High illuminating the way, it would be the right path to take. If it is the wrong path, it is simply a lesson needed to be learned to get back on the right track.

Living a full life calls for courage to face whatever obstacle comes our way, failure and success go hand in hand, they go together like Siamese twins, success is not possible without failure. Romance the failure shadows of life, in order to embrace lasting success.

Pay attention to the inner voice, trust it, it is right especially when the heart is guided by the spirit of The Perfect Giving Being.

The redemptive power of giving and forgiving cleanses
false pride that mask insecurities and jealousies

Essence of Gratefulness

No one but the self can make the needed changes to move forward, being thankful for everything we are and what we have now is a restorative way of being that propels us forward even in the presence of uncertainty and trepidation.

Only the self can unleash the actions that bring peace or turmoil, it's all in our hands; choose, God granted us free will, and thank goodness for the ability to make mistakes, for the lessons learned and for the mending of fences.

The redemptive power of giving and forgiving cleanses false pride that mask insecurities and jealousies, and springs forth a generosity with self and others.

Be a giver even when not appreciated, is a way of telling God, I heard You, I surrender to Your will, and I am thankful!

It's about self awareness and making use of the
senses of smell, touch, sight, hearing and taste

It's About Being

It's about self awareness and making use of the
senses of smell, touch, sight, hearing, and taste; it is
about a state of being fully aware of other people
and your surroundings.

It is about moving your body to the pulsating sound
of a garawoun; to the drumming traditional Punta
beat; or to the Latin rhythms at a Zumba class.

It is about being fully aware of your touch; using
scented oils to gently, tenderly, and slowly massage
the aches and pains of the body.

It is about being aware and embracing the sound of
silence, which is the time for oneself to connect to
the spirit of the Most High.

It is about slowly eating fresh luscious strawberries
and savoring the sweet, tart juice in your mouth;
and even imagining giving a slow tantalizing kiss.

It is about embracing the spirit of the ancestors by
enjoying listening to Paranda music and the sound
of the drums and guitar, transporting oneself to
Yurumein, the ancestral land and imagining their
joys as well as their trials and tribulations.

It is about being herself, a sensual Garifuna woman projecting self-confidence and being the one that every man desires for a wife and lover; it is about being his Valentine all year round.

Just restless, with nothing really important
to say, just wandering mind babbling

Blah, Blah, Blah

Just restless, with nothing really important to say, just a wandering mind babbling blah, blah, blah...

No inspiration, just a mind barren of anything of consequence, maybe it could be like a hit song? Devoid of meaning like the popular things that are perceived as important, it's just blah, blah, blah...

Dehydrated of inspiration, dry like a barren terrain, that will start again at sundown, maybe then like in a desert, my mind will produce cool breezes, words of inspiration not just blah, blah, blah.

Maybe times like this are needed to fertilize the psyche and imagination, just like cow manure enriches the soil for planting, blah, blah, blah is needed now to enrich the top soil of the imagination.

Garifuna music is like an elixir for the soul

Garifuna Music

Garifuna music is like an elixir for the soul, the mystic sound of the drums takes you to another time and place, at times it feels as if our ancestors are calling, trying to get our attention and warning us of impending danger of losing our souls, but at the same time it is the anchor we need to pursue our dreams.

Throughout the years and many tribulations we still have survived and the times we've thrived, so we rejoice and go with the flow of our sound, letting the music soothe our souls, and let our bodies flow with the rhythm of our songs.

BAHHHH

It is a great displeasure and disappointment to believe
in someone that turns out to be nothing but a wolf in
sheep's clothing

Spirit of Deception

Our most important purpose in life is to help others, and if unable to help; at least do as the Hippocratic Oath for physicians dictates, at least "do no harm" and do not hurt others, as the Dalai Lama wisely advises. It is a great displeasure and disappointment to believe in someone that turns out to be nothing but a wolf in sheep's clothing pretending to need help, acting as if they are your friend, a con artist with predatory intentions looking for a target to use and abuse to inflict emotional pain.

Taking kindness for weakness, for stupidity, just for the pleasure of deception, this actor extraordinaire gloats for having the ability to manipulate and create a reality that brings out compassion to a fictitious situation that was created for the main purpose of controlling feelings and manipulating reactions, that is the mark of a wolf in sheep's clothing.

Do not let them anywhere near you; they are master manipulators, their mere presence is toxic, destroys love, trust and compassion. Pray for discernment to have the ability to steer clear of involvement in such spiritual warfare.

Beware of false prophets, which come to you in sheep's clothing, but inwardly they are ravening wolves. - Matthew 7:15

I am walking into the unknown with faith

Leap of Faith

I am walking into the unknown with faith as my companion, into a place that appears to have the absence of light, but continue to walk in faith, not knowing how everything is going to turn out.

In this journey I am walking alone, wishing that someone else was there with me, but fate had it that it will not be, as much as I wanted it to be, I have no control, so I must continue and do my best, praying for divine intervention and the guidance of the spirit of my ancestors to inspire me.

I am taking a leap of faith by walking into a place that I have never been. The exterior calmness is covering the fear and the overwhelming excitement of how close and yet so far I am in completing my quest.

The obstacles are many, and at times appear insurmountable, by taking a leap of faith the answers are appearing like steps in the air that materialize as I need them to get to the other side. Those steps in the air remind me of the footprints of God carrying me.

...my spirit was feeling
    so close to God's work of art...

Spirit of Peace

There is a need of the human psyche to occasionally refresh our minds, bodies and spirits. It can be done by reading a positive book that will heal your soul, take your mind to a far and peaceful place and let your imagination flow freely. Listening to soul healing Paranda music or an Ave Maria, or being in the company of free spirited and well intentioned people that are seeking to improve their lives without harming anything or anyone.

All these elements and more, were incorporated in my trip to the mountains of Sedona and the Grand Canyon, I was in awe at what my eyes were seeing and my spirit was feeling, so close to God's work of art.

Cruising the Colorado River, the mountains are alive even though they have been there for thousands of years, the patina created by years of existence appears like shadows of the spirits of the original people, the native Americans. As I gazed into the horizon I imagined the brave warriors defending their territories against the invaders, but also sharing the land the universe has provided: no fences, free, and open for everyone to share. Their spirit is ever present and not demanding "we want our country back".

There are always days like this,
it is possible that they are necessary

Pondering

My mind is racing, unable to concentrate on anything; nothing in particular is bothering me, just wondering from one thought to another, not feeling anxious, just flighty I guess.

There are always days like this, it is possible that they are necessary, like a mental cleansing, or maybe just to stop and look around you, get in touch with oneself and others, who knows? I think that this day will not be very productive, I guess that is what happens when you are always multi-tasking, now I am just wasting time writing what I would normally consider nonsense.

But it feels good, relaxed, it's like doodling if I only knew how to draw, so instead I am just writing random thoughts.....pondering...

Do not promise me anything,
just show me

Just Show Me

Do not promise me anything, just show me.

Dreams and visions without actions are only illusions.

Make them come true, just show me.

Do not tell me, you will do this and will to that, just show me.

Having a brilliant mind and a procrastinating attitude will not help you to just show me.

Do not promise me the moon and the stars; just show me the best you can do.

Put aside your fears of success, take a calculated risk, and just show me.

Grab a hold of an ounce of discipline and another ounce of courage; and say to yourself;

I will show you!

There
You
Are

At this moment,
    We are exactly where we need to be

At this Moment

At this moment, we are exactly where we need to be, we have made a choice, be it good or bad. Was it based on a whim or a well thought out plan? We are exactly where we need to be.

Was it based on a mirage due to a perceived desert of our life? We are exactly where we need to be. Was it based on a calculated risk, or we impatiently "jump off a plane without a parachute"? We are exactly where we need to be.

Our Creator has given us free will to follow His path or ours, whichever we choose; we are exactly where we need to be.

Marching to the beat of my internal drum...

Surrender

Marching to the beat of my internal drum, like our ancestors listening to my internal voices to provide direction and guidance, keeping the faith that with divine intervention, everything will work out as it is supposed to.

Seeking, taking action, and waiting without desperation, because I know, that if my deepest desire is in accordance with the will of God, it is already granted.

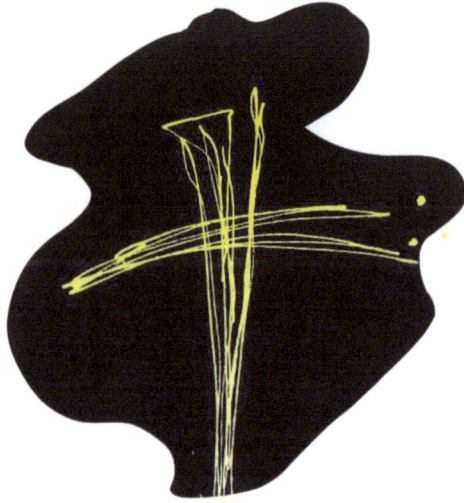

Ash Wednesday, a symbol of renewal, the beginning
of Lent; forty plus days before Easter, a time of
preparing for the resurrection of our Lord Jesus Christ

Ash Wednesday

Ash Wednesday, a symbol of renewal, the beginning of Lent; forty plus days before Easter, a time of preparation for the resurrection of our Lord Jesus Christ which culminates on Easter Sunday.

During this Lent season, I am not giving up anything in particular; instead I am striving to become the human being that The Creator intended me to be. In becoming that, it will require a heart and mind transformation towards self and others; a thirst for righteousness and hunger for justice for our Garinagu people, and hoping and praying for unity during the times of economic warfare.

I hope to journey to the wilderness of life in the company of the Most Holy, to move beyond the ordinary and discover my sacred purpose. I am willing to live without knowing and taking action while patiently waiting for divine intervention, until I return to the beginning, ashes to ashes...

...the flame of hope
still burns brightly in their lives...

Fullness of Life

Desiring to bring back the feeling of fullness of life, saying good bye to that annoying feeling of emptiness as if something is lacking; not happy, not sad, not angry, not lonely, not content, just restless, with a sensation that something is missing, and needing to be filled with something You want, that I am yet to know.

Is it a lack of desire? Is it lack of clear goals? Is it deficiency of efforts? No, all those essentials are there, just need to execute, I accept as true that I am looking for people I can trust, that can see the godly vision, and fulfill the divine plan that You placed in my mind.

I must recapture that feeling of fullness within myself, regardless of who is there in the sidelines, sometimes hot, sometimes warm, and most of the time radiant in their absence. I am not giving up, I will find the right ones, the seekers, the dreamers that although having been in the desert, the flame of hope still burns brightly in their lives. Those like-minded souls that the universe will unite to manifest Your divine plan.

Dear Father in heaven, please have mercy on your servant, position me in the right path, and fill my spirit with Your Spirit, so as to never thirst for the lack of inspiration, and fill the desert of life with the eternal oasis of your mercy and love.

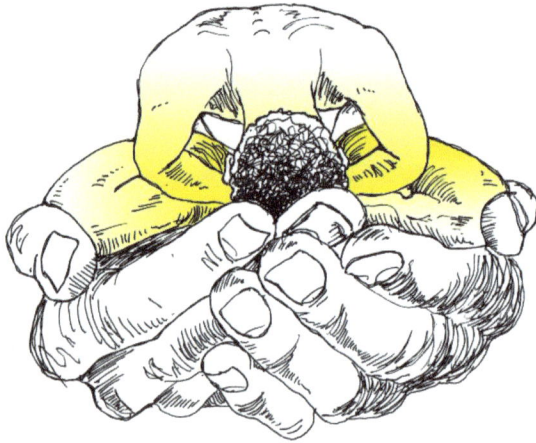

Missing the warmth of your arms
Holding me at this moment

Carry Me Now

Missing the warmth of your arms holding me at this moment, feel vulnerable and sad; it's times like this, that I need more from you, and I cannot get what a disease has stolen from you...

I am feeling sad, my man has lost his zest for life to a dreadful disease, unable to give me the emotional support in my time of need. Feeling alone and gloomy, just wondering who will care and support me in my time of need. Only God the All Knowing knows and will comfort me.

Others profess their love with hollow words missing the spice and seasoning of a loving emotional support, that would comfort my spirit like no food could supply, it is the emotional support that matters, just to be embraced lovingly will fill my soul with the food that my heart needs right now, I dream and wish for something that no human being could provide.

Oh how I need that one that would fill my soul now, that will hold me until I gain my strength, I am only dreaming, since the only one that could carry me now is the one and only, my Lord and Savior, I will rest my head on His shoulders as a little lamb that He loves so much.

Our Father who art in heaven do not let sorrow devour my spirit, do not let apprehension eat away at my hope, give me the heart to be the person You created me to be. Let me look in the mirror of Your love, with humility, and I will give You my burdens that only You my Lord and Savior can carry me now.

Whether times are good or bad,
loving you does not change

Letter to my Father

Whether times are good or bad, loving you does not change, time makes no difference, it has been over fifty years since your passing, God wanted you to go ahead of you wife and children, however, even though I was a child, or maybe because of it, I have always felt your presence in my life.

On the day of my wedding, missed you walking me down the aisle, giving me away to the man that would become my husband, and love me and cherish me, nor did I had the opportunity to have a dance with you, but God in his divine wisdom, had my older brother, your namesake, be there to stand for you. I missed you when I graduated from college, also when my sons were born, did not have the fortune to have their grandpa hold them and kiss them to welcome them to the world. But again, God in His immense wisdom, gave me my husband, there with me to welcome each one of our sons coming into the world.

You lived before your time, loving, compassionate, smart, handsome, charismatic and generous; those are some of the words that I heard through the years to described you; making a big difference in the lives of so many.

Your daughters were saved by a man that remembered what you did for him and others in our community; he was moved to take over the navigation of a boat caught in a storm in the middle of the ocean, traveling from Santa Rosa Aguan to La Ceiba. The sight of seeing your two daughters terrified by the monster waves, he stepped in and with courage, determination and without hesitation stated, "the daughters of Salomon Guity are in this boat and we cannot allow this boat to sink", in that instance there you were watching over us, and with the divine intervention of the Most High, you were there to inspire this brave soul to be moved to save your daughters and the people traveling in that boat. The action of that man forever stayed etched in the heart of your daughter, and increased the awareness of the significance of kindness and giving freely.

You endured pain beyond understanding when you realized that you were leaving your wife and nine children behind, however, again God with his infinite wisdom, love and mercy, gave you a wife, that was a mother and a lioness of a woman, that kept us together and guided us to became the adults that were are today…a reflection of you and her.

History of my Garifuna Ancestors

The Garifuna are the only Black Indigenous people in the Americas; indigenous meaning having presence in the region before the arrival of the Europeans. Along with images in museums of Pre-Columbians cultures of 1200 B.C. - 1580 A.D. such as Mayan and Inca civilizations, as well as newly discovered Mayan murals depicting black indigenous people during this era.

Notable historians (i.e. Rudolph Windsor, Prof. Van Sertima) has determined that African explorers were in this hemisphere prior to Columbus' arrival to the "New World". Our origins are still yet to be fully or accurately determined, since current theory of our origins states that we originated in 1635 in Saint Vincent Grenadines (Yurumein) and were exiled to Roatan Honduras in 1797after losing a second war to the British, this is not a feasible timetable for a people to develop a language and culture worthy of the UNESCO May of 2001 declaration of the Garifuna Culture to be a Masterpiece of the Intangible Heritage of Mankind.

A more likely scenario of our genesis is that the Garifuna People are descendants from early African explorers from the Mali Kingdom (c. 1230 to c.

1600.) that arrived in the Americas in the Pre-Columbians era. According to The Arab-Egyptian scholar Al-Umari quotes Mansa Musa the tenth Mansa and Emperor of the Malian Empire (c. 1280 - c. 1337) as follows:

"The ruler of the Ancient Mali Empire Mansa Musa, wanted to reach that (end) and was determined to pursue his plan. So he equipped two hundred boats full of men, and many others full of gold, water and provisions sufficient for several years. He ordered the captain not to return until they had reached the other end of the ocean, or until he had exhausted the provisions and water. So they set out on their journey. They were absent for a long period, and, at last just one boat returned. When questioned the captain replied: 'O Prince, we navigated for a long period, until we saw in the midst of the ocean a great river which flowed massively. My boat was the last one; others were ahead of me, and they were drowned in the great whirlpool and never came out again. I sailed back to escape this current.' But the Sultan would not believe him. He ordered two thousand boats to be equipped for him and his men, and one thousand more for water and provisions. Then he conferred the regency on me for the term of his absence, and departed with his men, never to return nor to give a sign of life".

The arrival of the ancient Mali explorers to the Caribbean Islands, and the subsequent intermarriage of the new explorers with the Caribbean natives, resulted in the creation of the new glorious culture of the Black Caribe, the GARIFUNA.

Since the exile of the Garifuna from our homeland of Yurumein to Roatan, in April 1797, without losing our language and culture, the descendants of these brave warriors today are doctors, certified public accountants, lawyers, professionals in various fields, artists, teachers, politicians, entrepreneurs, entertainers, international sports figures, laborers, and are fully integrated in the fabric of society in the United States, Honduras, Belize, Guatemala and Nicaragua, and many other countries throughout the world.

"AÑATEGO OO CHULUHAÑO, HABURUGAÑON WARAGAMA GAYO"... Here they come! Oh they have arrived! The ancestors are arriving... Dugu by Aurelio Martinez

NOTE

NOTES

NOTES

NOTES

NOTES

NOTES

NOTES

NOTES

NOTES

NOTES

----

www.ingramcontent.com/pod-product-compliance
Lightning Source LLC
Chambersburg PA
CBHW041529090426
42738CB00035B/16